THE REMINISCENT OBJECT

Paintings by William Michael Harnett
John Frederick Peto and John Haberle

LA JOLLA MUSEUM OF ART
July 11 through September 19, 1965
SANTA BARBARA MUSEUM OF ART
September 28 through October 31, 1965

Cover: "Old Time Letter Rack," 1894 by John F. Peto
Courtesy of the Museum of Fine Arts, Boston, Mass.

Library of Congress Card Catalogue No. 65-26203

LENDERS TO THE EXHIBITION

Mr. and Mrs. James W. Alsdorf, Winnetka, Ill.
Mrs. John W. Barnes, Silvermine, Norwalk, Conn.
Dr. and Mrs. Irving Burton, Huntington Woods, Mich.
Mme. Vera Haberle Demmer, New Haven, Conn.
Mr. and Mrs. Lawrence A. Fleishman, Detroit, Mich.
Mr. Albert Frankenstein, San Francisco, Calif.
Mrs. Avis Gardiner, Stamford, Conn.
Mr. and Mrs. Martin Grossman, New York, N. Y.
Mr. and Mrs. Frank T. Howard, Bryn Mawr, Pa.
Mr. Oliver B. Jennings, New York, N. Y.
Mr. and Mrs. Cheston Keyser, Island Heights, N. J.
Mr. and Mrs. Howard Keyser, Philadelphia, Pa.
Mr. and Mrs. James M. B. Keyser, Philadelphia, Pa.
Dr. and Mrs. Irving Levitt, South Field, Mich.
Mr. W. C. Munnecke, Leland, Mich.
Mr. and Mrs. Meyer P. Potamkin, Philadelphia, Pa.
Mr. Marvin Preston, Fern Dale, Mich.
Mr. Oscar Salzer, Los Angeles, Calif.
Mrs. Gloria Shiner, East Haven, Conn.
Mr. and Mrs. Victor Spark, New York, N. Y.
Mr. Mortimer Spiller, Buffalo, N. Y.
Mr. William J. Williams, Cincinnati, Ohio
Arizona State University Collection of American Art, Tempe, Ariz.
Boston Museum of Fine Arts, Boston, Mass.
Butler Institute of American Art, Youngstown, Ohio
Chicago Art Institute, Chicago, Ill.
Columbus Gallery of Fine Arts, Columbus, Ohio
Denver Art Museum, Denver, Colo.
The Detroit Institute of the Arts, Detroit, Mich.
Flint Institute of Arts, DeWaters Art Center, Flint, Mich.
Munson-Williams-Proctor Institute, Utica, N. Y.
New Britain Museum of American Art, New Britain, Conn.
Newark Museum of Art, Newark, N. J.
Pennsylvania Academy of Art, Philadelphia, Pa.
Philadelphia Museum of Art, Philadelphia, Pa.
The Phillips Collection, Washington, D. C.
Santa Barbara Museum of Art, Santa Barbara, Calif.
Smith College Museum of Art, Northampton, Mass.
Springfield Museum of Fine Arts, Springfield, Mass.
Wadsworth Atheneum, Hartford, Conn.
Hirschl and Adler Galleries, New York, N. Y.
Knoedler and Co., Inc., New York, N. Y.

CORRIGENDA

In the Introduction, the reproduction now numbered 14
should be numbered 15.
In the catalogue listing, the dimensions of 16½ x 20
now shown for item number 13 should be 9¼ x 12¼.
In both the catalogue listing and in the section of
reproductions, item number 46 should be titled
"Lincoln and the Phleger Stretcher, 1898," rather
than "Lincoln and the Phleger Stretch, 1898."

ADDENDUM

To the catalogue listing should be added:

67   Still Life, John F. Peto
     Oil on canvas, 21½ x 29½
     Hirschl & Adler Galleries, New York, N.Y.

FOREWORD AND ACKNOWLEDGMENTS

The paintings of William Michael Harnett (1848-1892), John Frederick Peto (1854-1907) and John Haberle (1856-1933) have never been seen to any degree in Southern California, nor have they been associated together in a single exhibition of this scale before this time.

As it sometimes happens, art has within it the power to evoke a re-assessment of the value of its own past. With the prodding and spade-work of two unusually perceptive people this is exactly what has happened with the work of our three painters. When in 1939 Edith Halpert in her Downtown Gallery presented the paintings of Harnett in an exhibition entitled "Nature-Vivre" she stunned the art world for this was the first time this painter's work had been seen in any depth and very possibly to any extent even been exhibited publicly for nearly forty years. Innocently and unknowingly several paintings by John F. Peto were also part of this show as they were signed with Harnett's name and at the time there wasn't an expert alive who could tell the difference. The other person to whom we are indebted is Alfred Frankenstein whose personal interest stemmed from the "Nature-Vivre" exhibition and was soon supported by a research grant to document the life and work of Harnett. Not only did he achieve this goal but, in the process discovered the superb and hitherto forgotten painters Peto and Haberle and, in addition, a whole tradition of American precisionistic still life painting, which had apparently passed from conscious memory.

Bringing this exhibition to the West Coast and presenting it in light of recent and especially contemporary aesthetic developments such as the assemblage-collage, pop art and strong "return-to-the-object" movements are then the reasons for this exhibition.

From the very outset, this exhibition has been dependent upon the knowledge of Alfred Frankenstein. Without his genuine interest, encouragement and cooperation any attempt to assemble these paintings into a coherent grouping would have been impossible. He deserves my most sincere thanks for his patience, enthusiasm and guidance.

It is a privilege to convey my appreciation and that of the Trustees of the La Jolla Museum of Art and the Santa Barbara Museum of Art to those people, collectors, museums and galleries whose understanding and assistance have made this exhibition a reality.

Organizing this exhibition involved the effort and dedication of numerous people. I am most grateful to Dr. Thomas W. Leavitt, Director of the Santa Barbara Museum of Art for his help and interest, to Mr. James Alsdorf for making it possible to reproduce Harnett's "Golden Horseshoe" in color, to Mr. William Steadman, Director of the University Art Gallery, University of Arizona for his arranging for the use of the color negatives for Harnett's "Rack," to Mr. Lynn G. Fayman and to Mr. John Waggaman for their critical help in photographing the paintings which appear in this catalogue and to members of our museum staff for their dedication and contribution to the preparation of the exhibition and catalogue.

Donald J. Brewer, Director
La Jolla Museum of Art

INTRODUCTION

"As our taste expands, the past grows with it, somehow always ahead." So said James Thrall Soby in a piece he published when he was art critic of the Saturday Review. The present exhibition signalizes some phase of that growth. It is the first exhibition ever held to concentrate on the three giants of American still life painting at the end of the 19th century: William Michael Harnett, John Frederick Peto, and John Haberle.

Twenty years ago only the name and work of Harnett were known. Ten years ago that neat, simple picture was most confusedly shattered, as the result of research by the writer of these lines, with the sudden emergence from the past of a whole, large school of American still life painters who had been totally forgotten. Today, while interest is still justifiably high in the work of artists like Jefferson David Chalfant, Richard LaBarre Goodwin, and George W. Platt, we are able, as formerly we were not, to see the difference between the peaks and the hills.

The perspective of time has given us a trio of three major American still life specialists — Harnett, Peto, Haberle — similar in its own way to the more broadly contrasted trio of Homer, Ryder, and Eakins who were their contemporaries. The perspective of time also permits us to re-evaluate these artists and give each the distinctive place which his individuality demands.

Two traditions were of special importance in forming the personality of William Michael Harnett. One was the tradition of craftsmanship to which all of his family subscribed. His father was a shoemaker, his brother a saddle-maker, his sisters seamstresses; and William Michael began his own career as an engraver in the silversmithing shops of New York and Philadelphia. He grew up in the latter city and there came into contact with the second of the major traditions that moulded him.

In the first quarter of the 19th century, Raphaelle Peale of Philadelphia evolved a very distinctive still life style — small in scale, extremely precise in drawing, exploiting the appeal of simple, commonplace, humble objects arranged in a generally pyramidal fashion on a bare table-top against a background of empty space, with very heavy emphasis on the contrast between the surface textures of the objects depicted — glassware, porcelain, stoneware, fruits, and things made of metal and wood. Harnett begins precisely where Raphaelle Peale leaves off, but — and mark this well — half a century later.

Peale died in 1825. Harnett began to paint in 1874. His taste was half a century behind that of his time, and this is a fact of crucial importance with regard to him and the entire school to which he belonged. These painters were old-fashioned; they appealed to an audience whose standards were long out of date, and for this reason they were either overlooked or derided by the criticism of their time. To assume, as many have in our own day, that their work is typical of the standards of their era is an historical error of catastrophic proportions.

Now and then — it doesn't happen often, but it does happen once in a while — an artist will fall so far behind the procession of his times as to perform a kind of circumnavigation in reverse and come back at the head of the procession as the latest thing. This is what happened in the case of William Michael Harnett in 1939. In that year he was re-introduced to the general public with an enormously successful exhibition at the Downtown Gallery in New York. He had died in 1892, and in the succeeding years his reputation, such as it had been, had gradually evaporated; by 1939 no one in the art world, at least, remembered him at all. But the precisionism of painters like Charles Sheeler and Charles Demuth and the surrealism of painters like Salvador Dali and Pierre Roy had created exactly the atmosphere of taste wherein Harnett's work, with its craftsmanly realism and its surrealistic overtones, would find acceptance.

The exhibition of 1939 was a huge hit, and Harnett was briefly accorded a unique position in American art history: he was regarded as a modern painter who had somehow strayed into the wrong century. Far from being thought old-fashioned, as had been the case in his lifetime, he was now discussed as if he had been a modern precisionist, cubist, and surrealist all rolled into one.

Modern appreciations of the artists of the past are, of course, extremely valuable, especially when they are contrasted with the evaluations made of them in their own time. In the case of Harnett, however, this contrast was never attempted, with the result that half of the paintings which established his new reputation in 1939 were not by him at all, but by other artists of his time, and bore forged Harnett signatures. Some of these are still on the paintings in the present show.

Harnett's career was short. It lasted only 18 years and falls into three six-year periods — 1874 to 1880, mostly in Philadelphia; 1880 to 1886, in Europe, principally in Munich; 1886 to the artist's death in 1892, entirely in New York.

The first period is especially one of small, Peale-like, table-top still lifes stressing such humble subject matter as a mug, a pipe, and a newspaper or books, an inkwell, a quill pen, and a partially legible letter. But Harnett dealt with other subjects, too, in this first period, and it reaches its climax with the great *Artist's Card Rack* of 1879 (No. 10).

10   The Artist's Card Rack
      William M. Harnett

This represents an old but not very common still life tradition which can be traced back to the 16th century. Harnett's example of it — the only one he is known to have painted — is also a perfect example both of his abstraction and his surrealism. Mondrian himself could scarcely have made a more brilliant, asymmetrical composition of flat rectangles, while Rene Magritte or some similar surrealist might have conceived the idea, which Harnett exploits here, of addressing a whole series of postcards and envelopes to various people and then placing them under the tapes of the rack in such fashion that the crucial word or the crucial syllable is invariably covered; everything looks as if it ought to be legible and the painting hints at the slightly sinful pleasure of reading someone else's correspondence, but then it balks that pleasure by the fact that nothing can really be read in it at all.

Europe had a very profound effect on Harnett. He started his work there in 1880 with a series of table-top still lifes similar to the old ones in subject matter but entirely new in style: they are miniaturistic in size and sparkle throughout with free little highlights of paint. Harnett also worked with the human figure while he was in Europe, to a markedly greater degree than he had at home; but the most important changes, suggested in the present exhibition by such pictures as *A Study Table* (No. 12) and the several versions of *After the Hunt* (Nos. 14 and 15), are embodied in still lifes of considerable size.

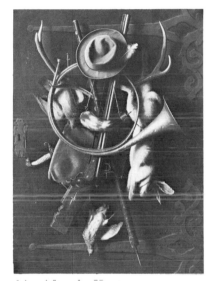

14   After the Hunt
      William M. Harnett

A new type of subject matter appears. Some simple objects remain, but now the scene is filled with things that look rare and expensive — armor, old tankards, medieval books, tapestries, Turkish rugs, jewel boxes, and so on. A strong vein of German romanticism manifests itself in the medieval guns and swords, the hunting horns, feathered hats, and elaborately hinged doors of *After the Hunt;* these paintings were, in all probability, adapted from a series of photographs by the famous Alsatian camera artist, Adolphe Braun.

Harnett ultimately painted more pictures of the type of *A Study Table* than any other. Here the objects are arranged on the table top in a specifically pyramidal fashion: they move backward and upward from the table's edge. This backward and upward movement is counterthrusted by the downward and forward motion of a newspaper, a sheet of music, or both, that hangs over the edge, and the edge itself acts as a kind of horizontal stabilizer for the whole. The background is no longer empty space but is boxed in by a panelled wall; often there is a deep, dark recess on the right-hand side. This formula is very common in the Dutch still life painting of the 17th century. It did not appear in Harnett until he went to Europe, and thereafter, as is observed above, he used it more often than any other. Obviously, he learned it in the European galleries.

12   A Study Table
      William M. Harnett

There is little or no change in Harnett's style after his return from Europe. His rate of production declined because of bad health; there were several years in the New York period when he painted little or nothing. The only shift of importance is in subject matter. He returns occasionally to an American vernacular type of theme — a big horseshoe (No. 18) or a *Faithful Colt* (No. 22). But the fancier subjects, the antiques and rarities, continue through this period as well.

18　Golden Horseshoe
William M. Harnett

44　Old Time Letter Rack
John F. Peto

These fancier subjects had great appeal for the collectors, old-fashioned in taste, who bought Harnett's pictures in his own time. The humbler subjects have more appeal for us today. Theoretically we of the present are not supposed to judge paintings by their subject matter, but in actuality subject is one of the things we take into account. Some aspects of Harnett therefore seem to us gaudy and excessively ornate — but whatever the subject, Harnett's work is full of the reminiscence of the American past, a past supposedly innocent, but revealed here as subtle, complex, and strangely magical.

As is pointed out above, a considerable number of paintings attributed to Harnett in the early days of the revival turned out on investigation to be works by obscure contemporaries to which Harnett's name had been forged. This fraud was committed by unscrupulous dealers in Philadelphia not long after Harnett's death, and no one now alive was involved in it. Harnett still had some reputation in those days, and pictures bearing his name could be sold for something; artists like John Frederick Peto, however, had no reputation at all and could scarcely give their paintings away; I have seen pictures by Peto bearing price tags of three and four dollars in the artist's own handwriting.

Peto had lived in the same general area as Harnett, had gone to school with him at the Pennsylvania Academy of the Fine Arts, had observed his success with interest, and had imitated a few of his motifs, notably the card rack and the mug-and-pipe picture. The forgery was therefore easy to commit. The method whereby it was detected was very complicated and cannot be discussed here; it is set forth in detail in my book, *After the Hunt,* (University of California Press, 1953). Once the distinction between Harnett and Peto is made, however, as it is in this exhibition, their styles seem so totally different that one finds it difficult to believe that any confusion between them could ever have existed. But one must add that while more paintings by Peto have been falsified as Harnett than works of any other artist, Peto is by no means the only painter whose work has been treated in this way. The "Harnetts" with forged signatures are by at least thirty different hands.

John Frederick Peto was born in Philadelphia in 1854, received his education there, and started to paint there in 1875. In 1889 he moved to Island Heights, New Jersey, and there he remained until his death in 1907. Island Heights was a camp-meeting town, and Peto went there primarily to lead the singing with his cornet. He painted in a haphazard, disorderly way, left piles of unfinished pictures, and gave away stacks of them to his neighbors. Harnett, by contrast, was an extremely systematic person. He finished everything and dated everything, and the progress of his style can be traced very clearly from year to year. Peto's work, on the other hand, is a shapeless heap, with relatively few clues as regards chronology.

Several things are clear, however. One of these things is that Peto is peculiarly the master of the rack picture. Harnett, apparently, painted only one such picture in his life, but Peto took his cue from it and painted dozens more. One of these, almost identical with No. 44 of the present exhibition, was given to the Museum of Modern Art in New York as a Harnett, has been reproduced more often than any other picture of its class, and is without much question the most famous rack picture in the world. Harnett reaped much unjust credit for this work for many years.

Peto is also a master of the simple, the commonplace, the humble, and the ordinary. He never painted the antiques and the fancy bric-à-brac of Harnett's middle and late years. This, I am convinced, was the main reason for his failure with the public in his own time and the main reason for his success with many elements of the public today.

Peto's drawing before Island Heights is likely to be somewhat loose, stringy, and confused. After 1880 his draftsmanship tightens considerably, and his paint takes on a soft, radiant, ground-glassy quality which has caused some to compare him to Vermeer. But Peto totally lacks Harnett's fascination with varied and contrasted textures. Where Harnett goes to extravagant length to differentiate between the tactile qualities of wood, paper, ceramics, fur, ivory, textiles, iron, silver, leather, fruit, skins, candle wax, and so on, Peto renders all these things in precisely the same texture; in other words, he is more concerned with purely pictorial values than with the imitation of natural appearances.

But the most striking characteristic of Peto's style, especially in contrast to Harnett's, is the baroque restlessness of his composition. Harnett's objects are by no means invariably at ease, but the whole effect of his work is eminently reposeful compared to the acrobatics of Peto. Except in his small table-top pictures, nothing is ever at rest in Peto's work; everything slides, falls, dangles, or balances in the most precarious and alarming fashion. His lighting, also, is intensely dramatic, picks up bits of this and spots of that and casts the rest into deep shadow. The objects he chooses to paint are not only commonplace but frequently torn, burned, ripped, or otherwise violated. There is a strong undercurrent of violence in his still life. In a sense he is a forerunner of Rauschenberg and other moderns who treasure the wasted and derelict objects of modern life. In spirit he also has strong ties with those other great American isolates of his own time, Homer, Ryder, and Eakins. John Frederick Peto, in other words, stands more in the main stream of American painting than does William Michael Harnett.

John Haberle has never been confused with Harnett and no works of his have ever been forged with Harnett's name, but he is of the same general school as the two other masters dealt with in this exhibition. He was born in New Haven, Connecticut, in 1856 and died there in 1933. He was a member of the technical staff at the paleontological museum of Yale University, and the 19th century controversies of science and religion are hinted in a number of his paintings, notably the irreverent *Time and Eternity* (No. 65), with its rosary beads, its playing cards, and its reference to Robert Ingersoll, the atheist preacher.

65   Time and Eternity
John Haberle

Haberle is especially the master of *trompe l'oeil* among the three painters of our show. He is the only one of the three who regularly, repeatedly, habitually — and most successfully — tries to fool the eye of the beholder into taking a painted representation of a thing for the real thing. He achieves this effect with a number of devices, but especially by avoiding deep space. In every Haberle of the current show, the eye is immediately stopped in its backward progress by a door, wall, or flat barrier of some kind. The objects hanging against this door, wall, or barrier are so modeled as to suggest that they protrude into the spectator's space (*Japanese Doll*, No. 60 or the above-mentioned *Time and Eternity*), or else they are entirely flat and are not modeled at all. A glance around the exhibition will demonstrate that Harnett and Peto also use these devices, and quite frequently, but they also exploit deep space, especially in their table-top still lifes. Haberle, however, never painted a table top in his entire career. Everything he did in the domain of still life is almost entirely two dimensional. Even when he paints the contents of *A Bachelor's Drawer* (No. 63), he depicts the objects fixed to the flat front of the drawer, in a most abnormal not to say impossible way, rather than inside it. There are sound psychological and physiological reasons for the avoidance of deep space and the emphasis upon flat objects on the part of eye-fooling "realists," but once again I must refer the reader to my book for a discussion of them; there is no room for that discussion here.

The need for the two-dimensional is, incidentally, the main reason for the persistent painting of paper money by all the artists of the present show. It has nothing to do with the value of the money as such; indeed, Haberle and his contemporaries frequently painted Confederate money, which had just been devaluated in their time and was the proverbial symbol of utter worthlessness at that period.

60   Japanese Doll (*detail*)
John Haberle

Haberle is the great vernacularist of 19th century American painting. He is actually the first pop artist, and a detailed look at a picture like *A Bachelor's Drawer* will reveal some astonishing parallels to the work of the modern pop-art school.

In the center of the painting, for example, is the lid of a cigar box, painted with the most fanatical detail in every curlicue of its engraved labels and revenue stamps. This is held to the drawer by means of a yellow ribbon looped around a nail at the top and two little leather hinges along the bottom edge. This hinged cigar-box lid is a crude container behind which are held a corncob pipe, an old comb, a small corked bottle, an envelope torn open at its right-hand end, a label or baggage check of some sort with a tasseled cord attached to it, and, at the extreme left-hand side, a loop of shoelace. Why does an artist

63   A Bachelor's Drawer (*detail*)   John Haberle

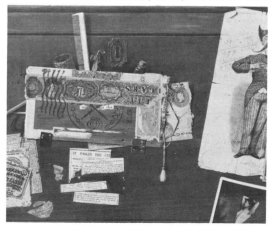

paint a conglomeration like that? He is, I think, debunking the high falutin'-ness of art, the notion that art must confine itself to a limited, "noble" subject matter and precious materials; as I put it in my book, "where some of his contemporaries fling their bold artistic challenge in the face of the vast grandeurs of the Rockies, Haberle fishes a comb, a ticket stub, or a canceled stamp out of his pocket and bids us marvel at *that*."

This is precisely the kind of debunking of cultural pretension that fills Mark Twain's books about his travels abroad; and both Haberle and Twain would have understood Alan Kaprow, critic and inventor of the Happening, when, in predicting where art would go after the death of Jackson Pollock, he said, "Objects of every sort are materials for the new art: paint, chairs, food, electric and neon lights, smoke, water, old socks, a dog, movies, a thousand other things which will be discovered by the present generation of artists." But the analogy between the passage in *A Bachelor's Drawer* just described and the painted Coca-Cola bottles and Campbell's soup cans of Andy Warhol is even more remarkable.

We have already mentioned paper money, of which there is much in *A Bachelor's Drawer;* it seems almost superfluous to add that the pop artists are painting paper money again, as well as the stamps and playing cards beloved of Haberle and his colleagues. The largest thing in *A Bachelor's Drawer,* is a cheap colored engraving of a dandy with fancy whiskers and hair-do. The analogy with Roy Lichtenstein and his pop-art emphasis on comic-book illustration is obvious enough. Haberle's bachelor liked cheap nudity, as witness the photograph so modestly draped with a band from a package of envelopes; the parallel to Mel Ramos and his pop-art cuties is clear. Going outside *A Bachelor's Drawer* it is worth observing that Haberle paints his own palette (No. 64); so does the pop artist, Jim Dine. Haberle paints street signs. So do pop artists as diverse as Robert Indiana and James Rosenquist. And it is scarcely news that a palette is as flat as a dollar bill and that practically everything painted by the pop artists is strictly two-dimensional; even the landscapes of Lichtenstein lack specific depth.

Haberle, like the pop artists, had a keenly satiric mind and a fine sense of the absurd. The parallels one can draw between his work and that of the present day confer a sense of historic continuity on the recent painting and reveal new, contemporary meanings in the old. To throw such bridges from past to present is one of the most important things an exhibition like this one can accomplish.

Alfred Frankenstein

64   The Palette   John Haberle

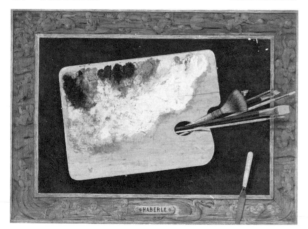

16 Still Life With Tankard, 1885
    Oil on canvas, 16½ x 20

CATALOGUE

Height precedes width in all dimensions. Dimensions are in inches. Lenders are credited on the final line of each entry.

WILLIAM MICHAEL HARNETT

1 Oil Sketch, 1874
   Oil on canvas, 8¾ x 5¾
   Mr. and Mrs. Alfred Frankenstein, San Francisco, Calif.

2 Oil Sketch, 1874
   Oil on canvas, 11-7/16 x 7-15/16
   Mr. and Mrs. Alfred Frankenstein, San Francisco, Calif.

3 Three Mounted Groups of Pencil Sketches for Still Life
   Pencil on paper
   Mr. and Mrs. Alfred Frankenstein, San Francisco, Calif.

4 Still Life — Five Dollar Bill, 1877
   Oil on canvas, 8 x 12⅛
   Philadelphia Museum of Art, Philadelphia, Pa.

5 Still Life, 1878
   Oil on canvas, 12 x 9⅞
   Mr. and Mrs. Martin Grossman, New York, N. Y.

6 American Exchange, 1878
   Oil on canvas, 8 x 12
   Detroit Institute of Arts, Detroit, Mich.

7 Writer's Table, 1878
   Oil on canvas, 14⅛ x 11⅞
   Private Collection, New York, N. Y.

8 Secretary's Table, 1879
   Oil on canvas, 14 x 20
   Santa Barbara Museum of Art, Santa Barbara, Calif.
   Preston Morton Collection

9 Quill and New York Herald, 1879
   Oil on canvas, 11 x 14⅞
   Mr. Oliver B. Jennings, New York, N. Y.

10 Rack Painting (The Artist's Card Rack), 1879
   Oil on canvas, 30 x 25
   Hirschl and Adler Galleries, New York, N. Y.

11 Still Life with "Telegraph," 1880
   Oil on canvas, 14⅛ x 20
   Denver Art Museum, Denver, Colorado

12 A Study Table, 1882
   Oil on canvas, 39⅞ x 51⅜
   Munson-Williams-Proctor Institute, Utica, New York

13 Still Life, 1882
   Oil on wood, 16½ x 20
   Flint Institute of Art, DeWaters Art Center, Flint, Mich.

14 After the Hunt, 1883
   Oil on canvas, 54½ x 35
   Columbus Gallery of Fine Arts, Columbus, Ohio

15   After the Hunt, 1884
     Oil on canvas, 55 x 40
     Butler Institute of American Art, Youngstown, Ohio

16   Still Life With Tankard, 1885
     Oil on wood, 16½ x 20
     Mr. and Mrs. Mortimer Spiller, Buffalo, New York

17   The Old Violin, 1886
     Oil on canvas, 38 x 24
     Mr. William J. Williams, Cincinnati, Ohio

18   Golden Horseshoe, 1886
     Oil on canvas, 15½ x 13½
     Mr. and Mrs. James W. Alsdorf, Winnetka, Ill.

19   Meerschaum Pipe, 1886
     Oil on canvas, 17 x 12
     Mr. and Mrs. Martin Grossman, New York, N. Y.

20   Still Life, 1887
     Oil on canvas, 24 x 20
     Mr. and Mrs. Meyer P. Potamkin, Philadelphia, Pa.

21   For Sunday's Dinner, 1888
     Oil on canvas, 37⅛ x 21⅛
     Art Institute of Chicago, Chicago, Ill.

22   The Faithful Colt, 1890
     Oil on canvas, 22½ x 18½
     Wadsworth Atheneum, Hartford, Conn. The Ella Gallup Sumner and
     Mary Catlin Sumner Collection.

JOHN FREDERICK PETO

23   The Artist's Card Rack, 1880
     Oil on canvas, 24 x 20
     Arizona State University Collection of American Art

24   Office Board for Christian Faser, 1881
     Oil on canvas, 24½ x 20⅛
     Mrs. John Barnes, Comstock Silvermine, Norwalk, Conn.

25   Old Souvenirs, 1881
     Oil on canvas, 26 x 21½
     Falsely signed William M. Harnett
     Oliver B. Jennings, New York, N. Y.

26   Box of Books, 1884
     Oil on canvas, 20 x 24
     Falsely signed William M. Harnett
     Private Collection, New York, N. Y.

27   Still Life, Tankard, Pipe, Matches and Biscuit, 1887
     Oil on canvas, 6¼ x 9⅜
     Dr. and Mrs. Irving Levitt, South Field, Mich.

28   Banana and Orange, Ca. 1887
     Oil on academy board, 5⅝ x 8⅝
     Mr. and Mrs. Howard Keyser, Philadelphia, Pa.

29 Oranges and Box of Candies, Ca. 1887
Oil on academy board, 5⅝ x 8½
Mr. and Mrs. Howard Keyser, Philadelphia, Pa.

30 Bowie Knife and Lantern, Ca. 1887
Oil on canvas, 20¼ x 10¼
Mr. and Mrs. Howard Keyser, Philadelphia, Pa.

31 Old Friends, Ca. 1887
Oil on academy board, 8¾ x 11½
Falsely signed William M. Harnett
Private Collection, New York, N. Y.

32 Pistol, Gate Latch and Powder Horn, 1887
Oil on canvas, 14 x 9⅝
Mr. and Mrs. Cheston Keyser, Island Heights, N. J.

33 Five Dollar Bill, Ca. 1889
Oil on composition board, 6 x 9¼
Mr. and Mrs. Oscar Salzer, Los Angeles, Calif.

34 Lamps of Other Days, Ca. 1890
Oil on canvas, 27 x 36
Mr. and Mrs. Howard Keyser, Philadelphia, Pa.

35 Still Life with Pitcher, Gravy Bowl and Candlestick, Ca. 1890
Oil on canvas, 14⅝ x 9½
Mr. and Mrs. Victor Spark, New York, N. Y.

36 Board with Lincoln Photograph, Ca. 1890
Oil on canvas, 22 x 16
Mr. and Mrs. James Keyser, Philadelphia, Pa.

37 Still Life (Patch Painting), Ca. 1890
Oil on canvas, 17 x 14
Dr. and Mrs. Irving Burton, Huntington Woods, Mich.

38 Student's Materials, 1890-1900
Oil on canvas, 20¼ x 16¼
Museum of Fine Arts, Boston, Mass.

39 After Night's Study, Ca. 1890
Oil on canvas, 14¼ x 20¼
Falsely signed William M. Harnett
The Detroit Institute of the Arts, Detroit, Michigan

40 Carpetbag, Hat and Umbrella, Ca. 1890
Oil on canvas, 19½ x 11½
M. Knoedler and Co., Inc., New York, N. Y.

41 Lard Oil Lamp, Ca. 1890
Oil on canvas, 14⅛ x 24⅛
Newark Museum of Art, Newark, N. J.

42 Fish House Door, Ca. 1890
Oil on canvas, 63 x 40
Pennsylvania Academy of Art, Philadelphia, Pa.

43 For a Sunday Dinner, 1893
   Oil on canvas, 30 x 22
   Mr. and Mrs. Howard Keyser, Philadelphia, Pa.

44 Old Time Letter Rack, 1894
   Oil on canvas, 30 x 25
   Museum of Fine Arts, Boston, Mass.

45 Things to Adore: My Studio Door, 1895
   Oil on canvas, 49½ x 29¼
   Santa Barbara Museum of Art, Santa Barbara, Calif.

46 Lincoln and the Phleger Stretch, 1898
   Oil on canvas, 10 x 14
   Mr. and Mrs. Howard Keyser, Philadelphia, Pa.

47 Old Reminiscences, 1900
   Oil on canvas, 30 x 25
   The Phillips Collection, Washington, D. C.

48 Discarded Treasures, Ca. 1904
   Oil on canvas, 22 x 40
   Falsely signed William M. Harnett
   Smith College Museum of Art, Northampton, Mass.

49 Office Board for John F. Peto, 1904
   Oil on academy board, 10½ x 12¼
   Mr. and Mrs. Oscar Salzer, Los Angeles, Calif.

50 The Cup We All Race 4, 1905
   Oil on canvas and board, 25⅝ x 21½
   Private Collection, New York, N. Y.

51 Still Life with Blue Envelope and Inkwell
   Oil on board, 4¼ x 6½
   Mr. and Mrs. Oscar Salzer, Los Angeles, Calif.

52 Still Life with Green Envelope and Inkwell
   Oil on board, 4¼ x 6½
   Mr. and Mrs. Oscar Salzer, Los Angeles, Calif.

53 Still Life with Skull, (Memento Mori)
   Oil on canvas, 18 x 24
   Mr. and Mrs. Oscar Salzer, Los Angeles, Calif.

54 Still Life with Oranges and Goblet of Wine
   Oil on academy board, 6⅛ x 9¼
   Mr. and Mrs. Frank T. Howard, Bryn Mawr, Pa.

55 Still Life
   Oil on academy board, 9 x 12
   Mr. and Mrs. Frank T. Howard, Bryn Mawr, Pa.

56 Still Life with Mug, Pipe, Book and Candle
   Oil on canvas, 8¾ x 5¾
   Mr. and Mrs. Alfred Frankenstein, San Francisco, Calif.

JOHN HABERLE

57   Peanuts, 1887
     Oil on canvas, 8½ x 19¾
     Mr. W. C. Munnecke, Leland, Mich.

58   Changes of Time, 1888
     Oil on canvas, 24 x 20
     Mr. Marvin Preston, Fern Dale, Mich.

59   Can You Break a Five?, 1888
     Oil on canvas, 7¼ x 11
     Dr. and Mrs. Irving Levitt, South Field, Mich.

60   Japanese Doll, 1889
     Oil on canvas, 15½ x 6¼
     Mr. and Mrs. Lawrence A. Fleischman, Detroit, Mich.

61   The Clay Pipe, 1890
     Oil on canvas, 18 x 8¾
     Mr. W. C. Munnecke, Leland, Mich.

62   A Favorite, Ca. 1890
     Oil on canvas, 14½ x 11½
     Springfield Museum of Art, Springfield, Mass.

63   A Bachelor's Drawer, 1890-1894
     Oil on canvas, 20 x 36
     Mrs. Vera Haberle Demmer, New Haven Conn. and Mrs. Gloria Shiner,
     East Haven, Conn.

64   The Palette
     Oil on canvas, 17½ x 24
     Mr. Marvin Preston, Fern Dale, Mich.

65   Time and Eternity
     Oil on canvas, 14 x 10
     New Britain Museum of Art, New Britain, Conn.

66   The Slate, Leave Your Order Here
     Oil on canvas, 12 x 9½
     Mrs. Avis Gardiner, Stamford, Conn.

WILLIAM MICHAEL HARNETT
1848-1892

1   Oil Sketch, 1874
    Oil on canvas, 8¾ x 5¾

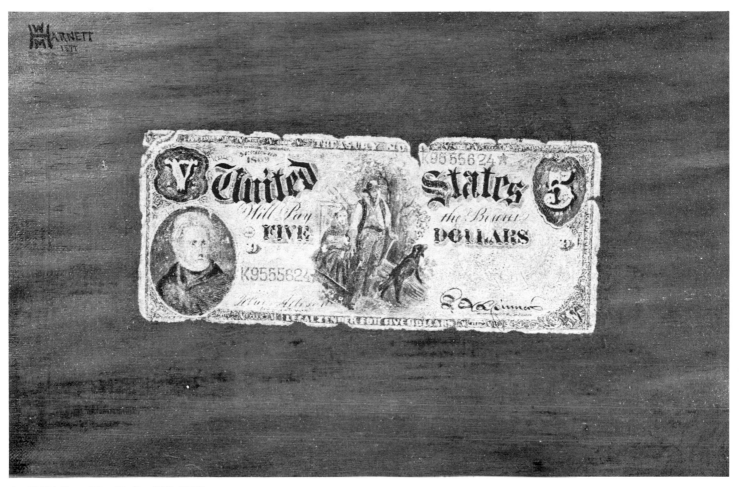

4 Still Life — Five Dollar Bill, 1877
   Oil on canvas, 8 x 12⅛

5   Still Life, 1878
    Oil on canvas, 12 x 9⅞

6   American Exchange, 1878
    Oil on canvas, 8 x 12

7   Writer's Table, 1878
    Oil on canvas, 14⅛ x 11⅞

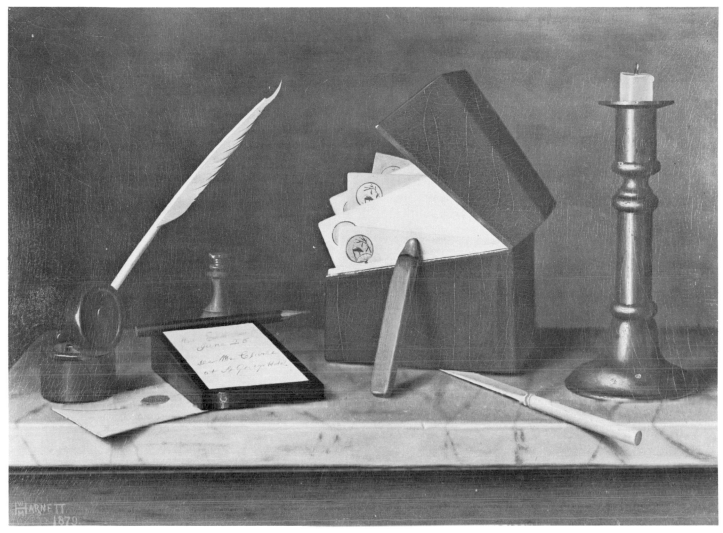

8 Secretary's Table, 1879
   Oil on canvas, 14 x 20

9   Quill and New York Herald, 1879
    Oil on canvas, 11 x 14⅞

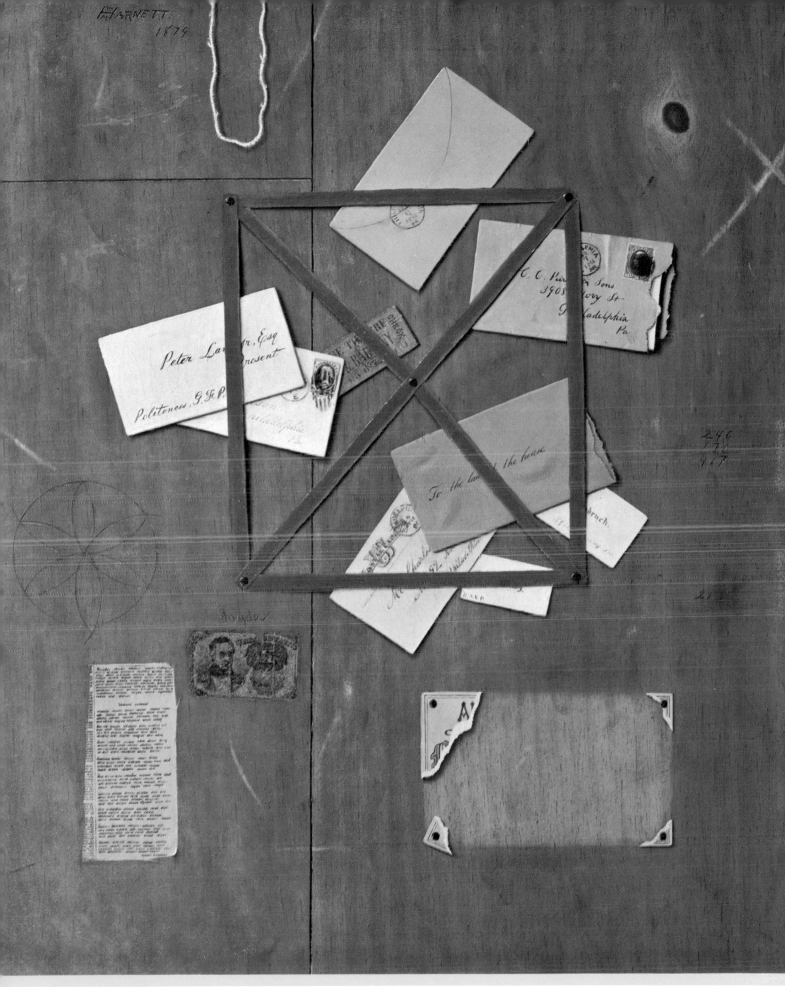

10   Rack Painting (The Artist's Card Rack), 1879
      Oil on canvas, 30 x 25

11   Still Life with "Telegraph," 1880
     Oil on canvas, 14⅛ x 20

13　Still Lite, 1882
　　9¼ x 12¼

12   A Study Table, 1882 *(detail)*
     Oil on canvas, 39⅞ x 51⅜

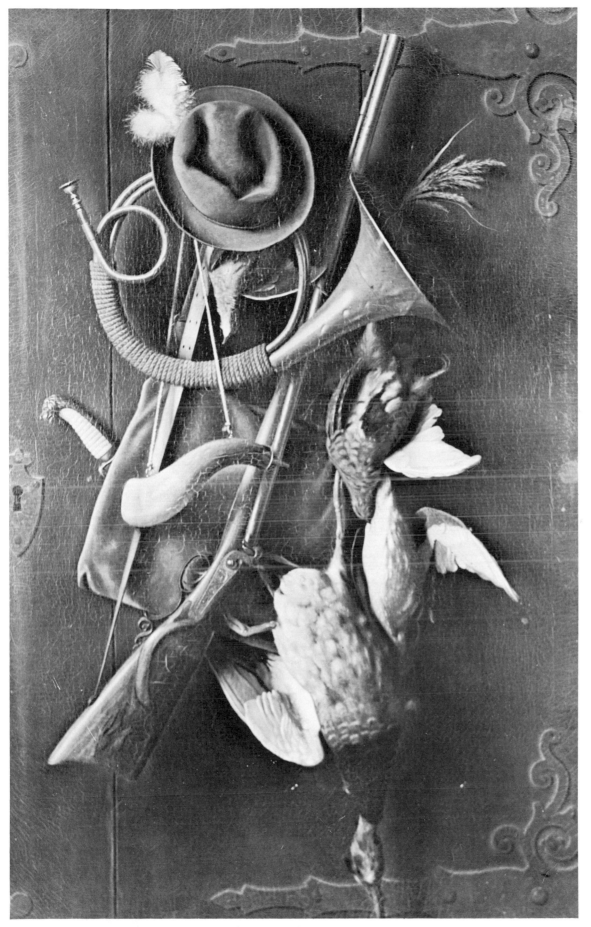

14   After the Hunt, 1883
     Oil on canvas, 54½ x 35

15   After the Hunt, 1884
     Oil on canvas, 55 x 40

18 Golden Horseshoe, 1886
Oil on canvas, 15½ x 13½

17   The Old Violin, 1886
    Oil on canvas, 38 x 24

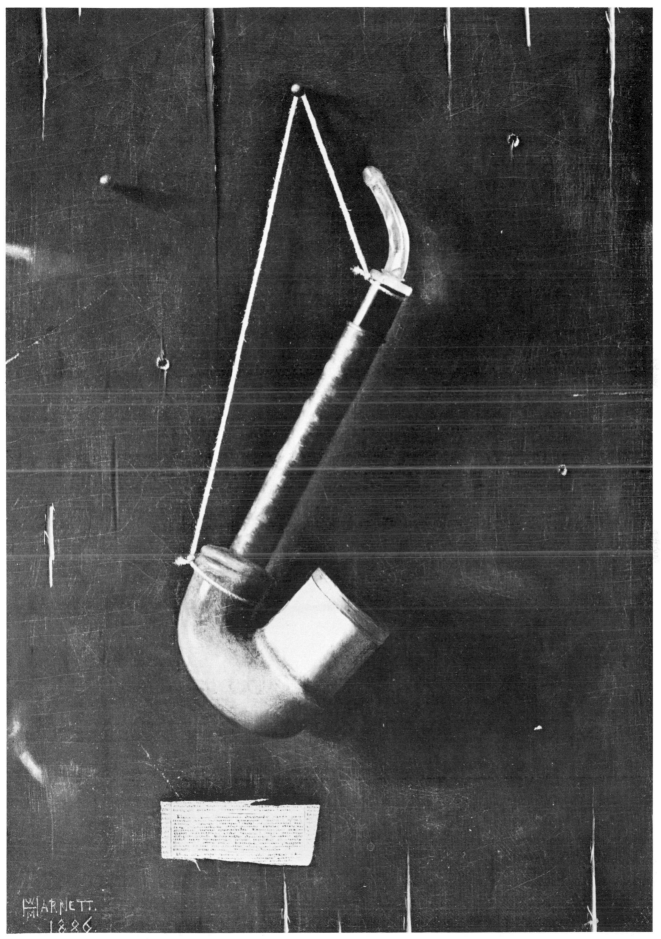

19 Meerschaum Pipe, 1886
    Oil on canvas, 17 x 12

20　Still Life, 1887
　Oil on canvas, 24 x 20

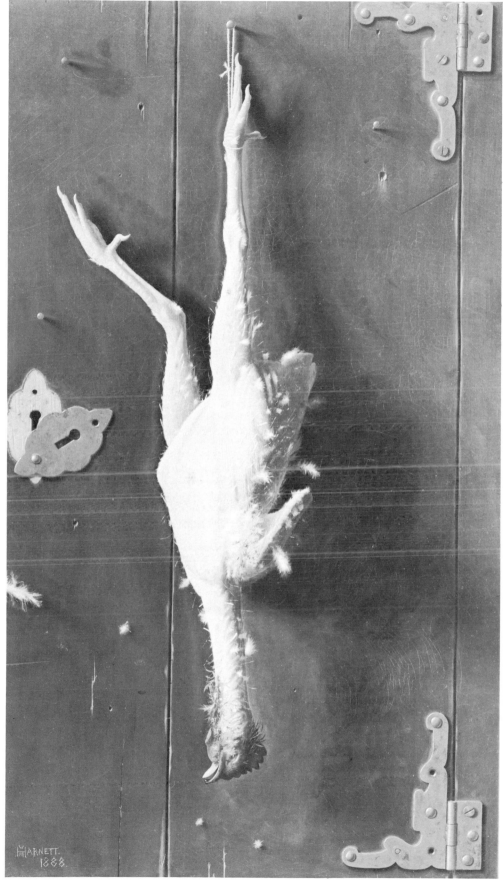

21   For Sunday's Dinner, 1888
     Oil on canvas, 37⅛ x 21⅛

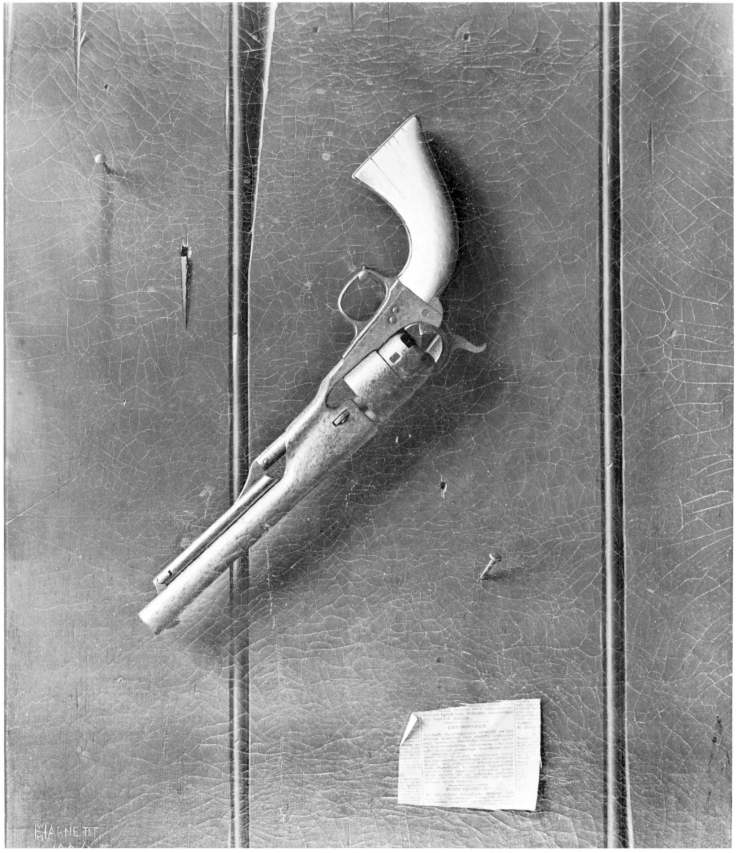

22   The Faithful Colt, 1890
      Oil on canvas, 22½ x 18½

JOHN FREDERICK PETO
1854-1907

23   The Artist's Card Rack, 1880
Oil on canvas, 24 x 20

24 Office Board for Christian Faser, 1881
Oil on canvas, 24½ x 20⅛

25   Old Souvenirs, 1881
     Oil on canvas, 26 x 21½

26 Box of Books, 1884
    Oil on canvas, 20 x 24

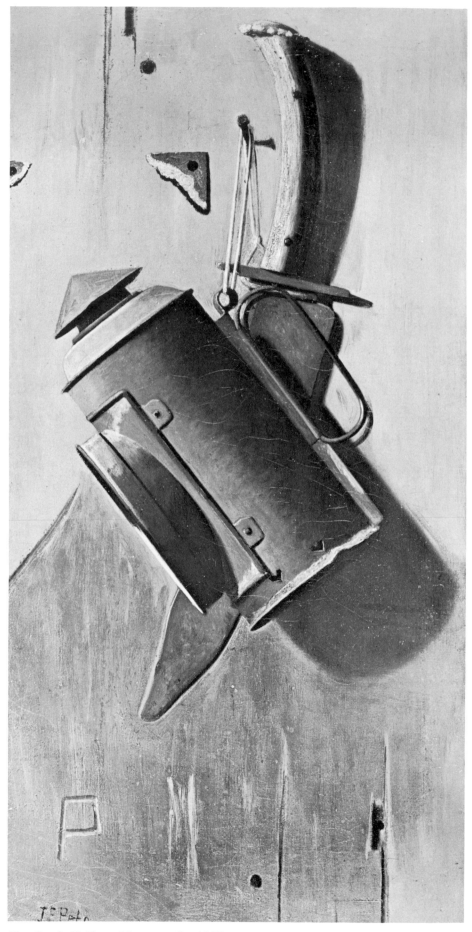

30 Bowie Knife and Lantern, Ca. 1887
Oil on canvas, 20¼ x 10¼

31 Old Friends, Ca. 1887
Oil on academy board, 8¾ x 11½

32   Pistol, Gate Latch and Powder Horn, 1887
     Oil on canvas, 14 x 9⅝

35   Still Life with Pitcher, Gravy Bowl and Candlestick, Ca. 1890
      Oil on canvas, 14⅝ x 9½

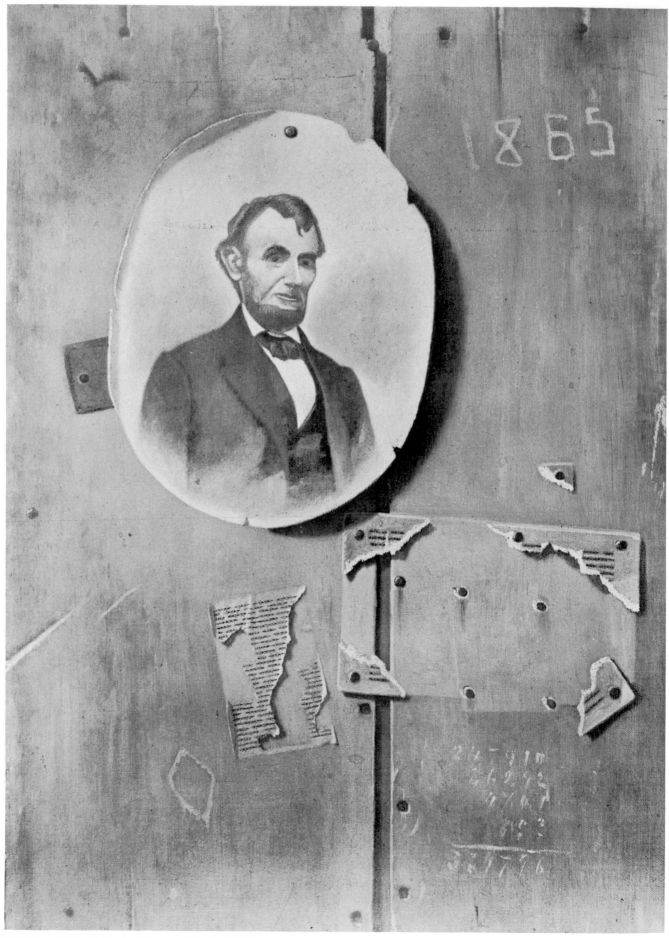

36   Board with Lincoln Photograph, Ca. 1890
Oil on canvas, 22 x 16

37   Still Life (Patch Painting), Ca. 1890
    Oil on canvas, 17 x 14

38   Student's Materials, 1890-1900
     Oil on canvas, 20¼ x 16¼

39   After Night's Study, Ca. 1890
      Oil on canvas, 14¼ x 20¼

41   Lard Oil Lamp, Ca. 1890
     Oil on canvas, 14⅛ x 24⅛

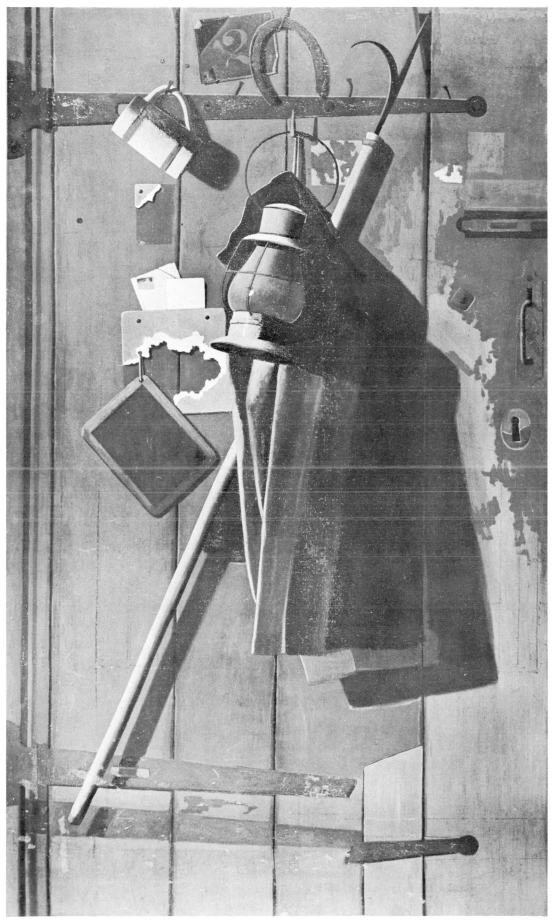

42 Fish House Door, Ca. 1890
Oil on canvas, 63 x 40

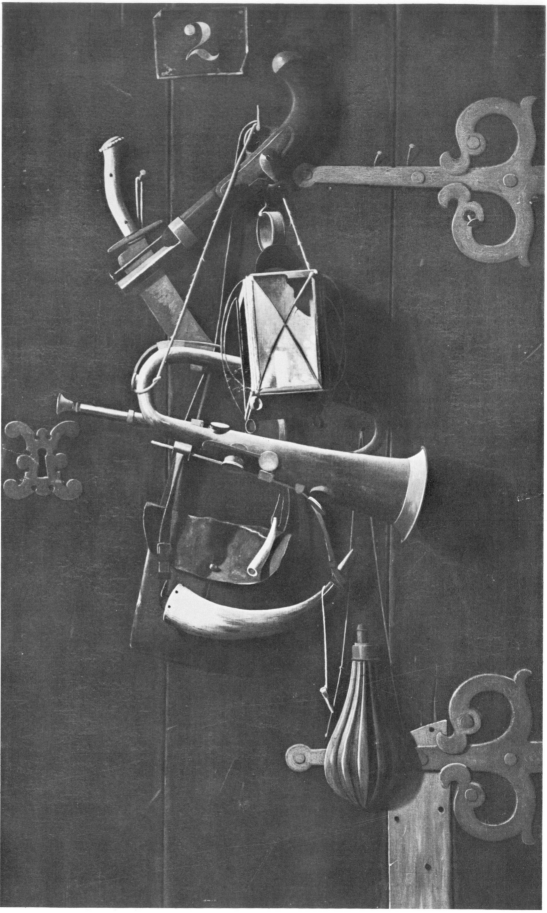

45   Things to Adore: My Studio Door, 1895
      Oil on canvas, 49½ x 29¼

46   Lincoln and the Phleger Stretch, 1898
     Oil on canvas, 10 x 14

47   Old Reminiscences, 1900
Oil on canvas, 30 x 25

48   Discarded Treasures, Ca. 1904
      Oil on canvas, 22 x 40

49 Office Board for John F. Peto, 1904
    Oil on academy board, 10½ x 12¼

50   The Cup We All Race 4, 1905
       Oil on canvas and board, 25⅝ x 21½

54 Still Life with Oranges and Goblet of Wine
Oil on academy board, 6⅛ x 9¼

JOHN HABERLE
1856-1933

63   A Bachelor's Drawer, 1890-1894
      Oil on canvas, 20 x 36

58   Changes of Time, 1888
Oil on canvas, 24 x 20

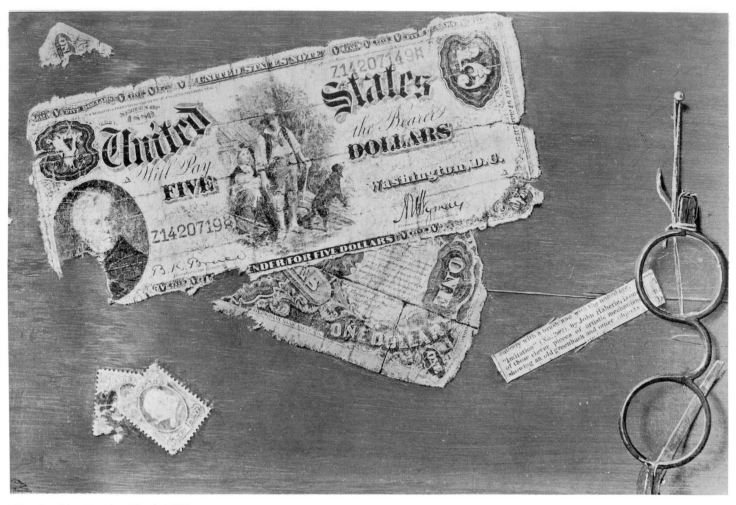

59 **Can You Break a Five?**, 1888
    Oil on canvas, 7¼ x 11

60 Japanese Doll, 1889
    Oil on canvas, 15½ x 6¼

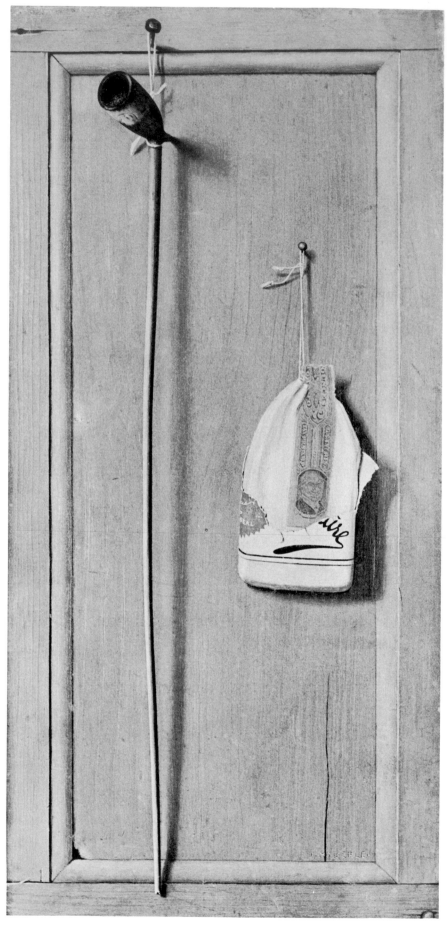

61 The Clay Pipe, 1890
Oil on canvas, 18 x 8¾

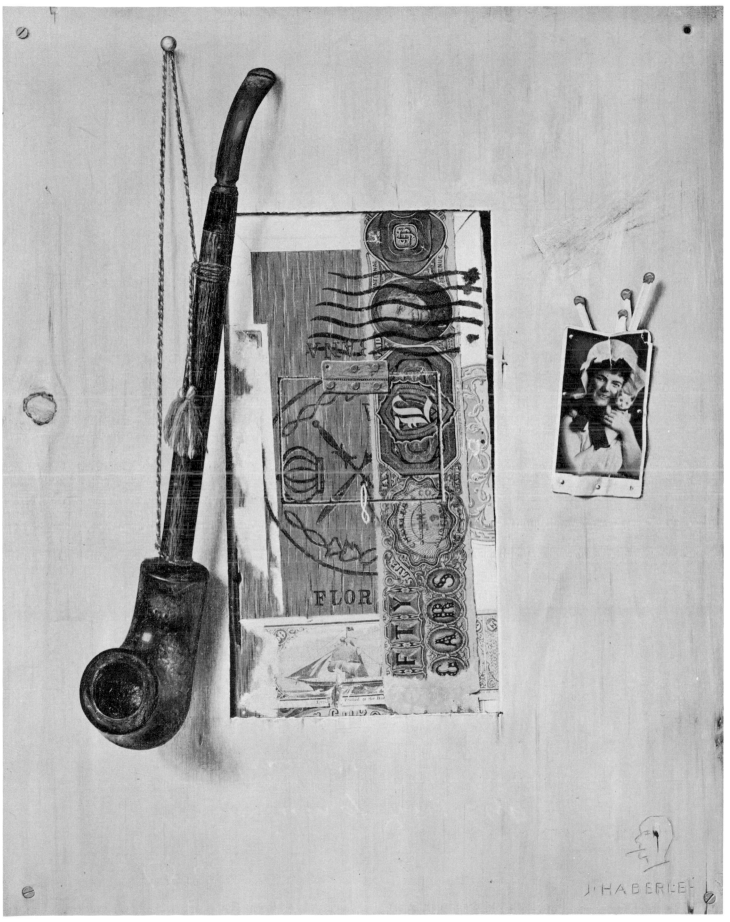

62   A Favorite, Ca. 1890
      Oil on canvas, 14½ x 11½

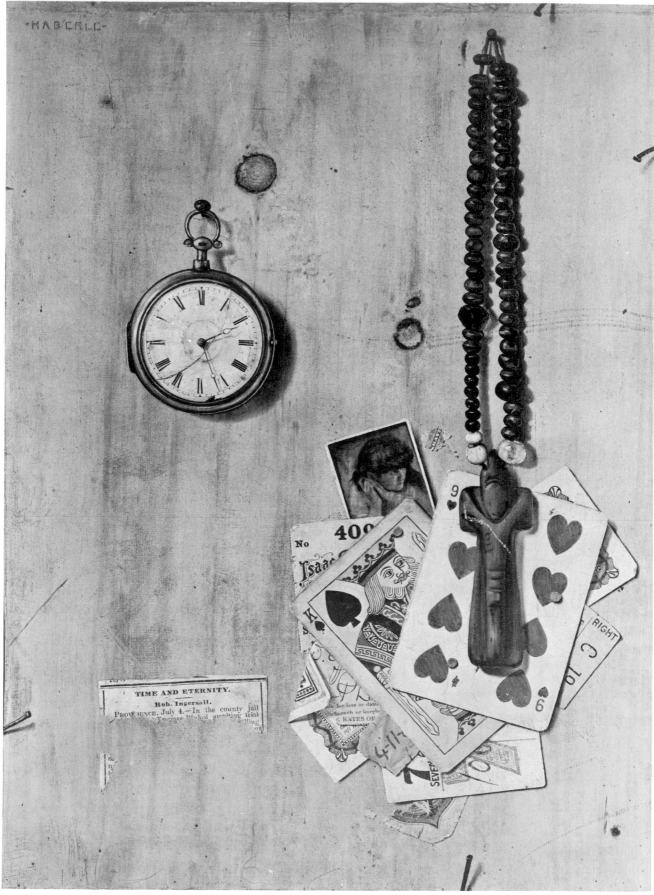

65 Time and Eternity
Oil on canvas, 14 x 10

66   The Slate, Leave Your Order Here
Oil on canvas, 12 x 9½

Design: La Jolla Museum of Art

                John Zane

Typography: Central Typesetting, Inc., San Diego

Printer: Conklin Lithograph, San Diego